# Firehouse Tales

## Stories by a Career Fire Fighter

## by

## Sam Stone

Firehouse Tales: Stories by a Career Fire Fighter
Copyright © August 15, 2017 by Sam Stone

FIRST EDITION
ALL RIGHTS RESERVED

ISBN-13: 978-1975643492
ISBN-10: 1975643496

Most of these stories are based upon truth, and rely solely upon the author's memory as to their accuracy. Some names, places, and incidents may have been altered somewhat for literary effect, and any resemblance to actual persons, living or dead, events, or locations is entirely coincidental.

Cover Illustration © Mechanik/Shutterstock
Hydrant Illustration © Air Vector/Shutterstock
Steam Engine Illustration © Hein Nouens/Shutterstock
Fire Fighter Illustration © PSV16/Shutterstock

# Table of Contents

# Introduction

Ever since I can remember, I wanted to be a Fire Fighter. My life as a Fire Fighter in Miami was the culmination of a dream. The memories I have of those times are represented, in some small part, in this collection of stories.

Growing up in Miami in the late 40s and 50s was like living in a children's paradise. Weekends and summers, we never had to go home for lunch because some sort of fruit was always ripe and easy to reach. We'd ride our bikes across the causeway to the beach and spend a few hours swimming and eating sea grapes. This was a large tropical plant with flat, stiff leaves up to ten inches in diameter, with clusters of grapes about three quarters of an inch in diameter. They had huge pits and very little fruit. We learned to open coconuts with our bare hands.

The old fire station at the north end of the town near where I lived (and eventually worked) was built in 1926. It housed an engine company and a ladder truck. It was the only station that didn't "transfer" to cover other stations when there was a large fire elsewhere, because of the railroad tracks. (One time, many years ago, the station was "transferred" into town to cover a station, when it received an alarm in that territory. They were unable to get to the fire because of a long train that had all the crossings blocked.)

Often, Fire Fighters in northern climates, after fighting fires, then have to chop the hose out of the ice. That wasn't our problem in Miami. Early in my career I was single with lots of time on my hands and, on my days off, I was a year-round swimmer. Summer visitors would complain about how warm the surf was. I'd say that's why the water is still warm enough for swimming during the winter.

Years later, with a family to provide for, I would occasionally take my lantern and dip net down to the seawall on the outgoing tide, hoping to catch enough shrimp for a meal. On rare occasions, you'd catch a "run" of shrimp (there'd be so many you could walk home on them). Runs didn't typically last all that long, but, if you were lucky, you could catch nearly a bucketful in almost no time at all. Next day on duty, the guys in the station would have peel-and-eat shrimp for dinner. The shrimp in

Biscayne Bay aren't very large (on occasion they get big enough to fry, but not all that often). Following a run, guys with huge nets they hauled behind their boats would be seen along the street selling shrimp from huge coolers.

I loved Miami, and I loved being a Fire Fighter.

I hope you enjoy my stories.


*Sam Stone*

# The Great Juke Box Fire

**There I was riding Engine Thirteen, when the bell rang** for a building assignment in the middle of the night, over on Northwest Second Avenue near Fifty-Fourth Street. I was on the tailboard with Big Al Lang and some rookie. Engine Thirteen didn't get all that many fires, and we were first in, with Engine Six not far away. Big Al and I were "cardiac kids," and the last thing we wanted was to lose that fire to those guys from over on Seventh Avenue.

This was in an older, two-story stucco building— one of those with a business downstairs, typically a grocery, pharmacy, or saloon. Upstairs there was usually a two-bedroom apartment, quite often originally occupied by the owner of the business. Sometimes there were two small apartments. This style of building was constructed during the boom, and almost all had parapet roofs, casement windows, and narrow outside stairways serving the apartments. Most often, they were on small lots, and the buildings were on the property line without setbacks. When the building was on a corner, the downstairs entrance to the business was quite often a set of double doors, on an angle facing the intersection, as did these. The downstairs in this building was a saloon that had been there all my life and probably from the building's inception.

Upon our arrival, the place was charged with smoke. Al pulled the jump line, while I put my breathing apparatus on. "Lieutenant Peanut Butter" assigned the rookie to hand drag a supply line to the hydrant on the corner, and I took the nozzle from Al so he could go for his air pack.

The place was hot and the smoke was heavy. It didn't take much time before I was on my belly, crawling forward toward the flames dancing back by the rear wall. In what felt like a few seconds, Al had returned, and I could tell from the sound of his breathing he had his air pack on and working.

We crawled back toward the fire only to find it wasn't a fire at all, but a juke box with lights flickering back and forth across the lower portion. I thought for a split second about pulling a quarter out of my pocket and playing a record, but then recalled it was the middle of the night and I wasn't wearing my uniform pants under my bunker gear. Oh, well, maybe next time.

Now, we had to figure out where the real fire was. Eventually, we found it in the office, behind the bar.

The next day on duty, the inspector dropped by and informed us it had been a friction fire—friction, that was, between the bar owner's wallet and the insurance policy. I gave thanks that the ceiling had held and no one in the apartments upstairs was injured or overcome with smoke.

I finally got tired of being in a station where the guys sat around all day waiting for an alarm that never rang, and transferred to another station with a busy engine company—but I'll always remember "The Great Juke Box Fire."

Sam Stone

# "Dolfin" Tale

**Weighing in at two hundred ten pounds, with a thirty-two inch waist,** a hell of a lot more muscle than common sense, AND, having two days off out of every three, it was easy to get into trouble. S-o-o-o-o, when Crazy Larry asked if I wanted to go fishing, I was all in.

Larry's aluminum boat was twelve feet long with a flat bottom, and definitely built for fishing in protected waters. The last time we had taken it out, we had a lot of fun in South Bay, catching lots of fish, so I was sure it would be another exciting day. We secured the boat to the top of Larry's station wagon, threw a small cooler (for beer), some rods, Larry's fishing box, bait bucket, and a cast net in the back, and were ready to go. When I asked about another cooler for fish, he said we wouldn't need one. I shrugged, and we took off.

This time, Larry put in at the north end so I assumed we were going fishing in North Bay.

Little did I know how wrong I was!

Once at the boat ramp, Larry walked along the sea wall, scanning the water for bait fish. Holding a portion of the cast net between his teeth, he would throw the net in a perfect circle, with the lead weights causing it to sink rapidly around a school of fish measuring three to four inches in length. It didn't take long to catch a few dozen, which I dutifully collected and threw into the bait bucket. All the while, Larry was spitting, in an effort to remove the brackish water from the line he held in his mouth while casting the net.

Motoring out of the protected ramp area, Larry pointed the boat through the cut toward the ocean. This cut, known as Baker's Haulover, empties almost the entire north end of Biscayne Bay, and the flow of water through that cut can be amazingly treacherous—especially on the outgoing tide. However, at the time, it was slack high tide and totally calm—AND there was no wind. Beyond the cut, the ocean outside was a sheet of glass as we motored into the morning sun. Before long, the buildings on Miami Beach had been reduced to about three to four inches in height at arm's length.

After a while, we saw seagulls diving at the water.

"Set up a couple of rods!" Larry shouted, as he gunned the little outboard motor and pointed the boat toward the gulls. It didn't take long before we reached the spot where they had been diving and . . . well . . . there was nothing. The gulls, however, were still circling overhead, and Larry was pounding the water with an oar and shouting at the fish, "Come on . . . I know you're there!"

When the gulls drifted a hundred yards or so away and began diving at the surface again, we cranked up and followed them. Throwing our bait overboard, we caught a half-dozen school dolphin (I always called them "dolfins"), measuring maybe eighteen inches or so in length. Not to be confused with the mammal, these dolphin were fish. Some folks call them "Mahi-mahi.

It works like this: Schools of larger fish feed on the schools of smaller fish, driving them to the surface. The gulls see the small fish, and start diving for breakfast.

I was amazed. There we were, alone with the gulls. We'd catch anywhere from a couple to a dozen fish; then the birds would move and we'd follow. Within an hour, two things happened: first, the bottom of the boat was full of fish; second, we were surrounded by party boats and professional fishermen. The nice thing was that we had far less difficulty following the gulls than did those huge boats filled with fishermen. As a result, we always got there first.

Finally, shading his eyes with one hand, Larry pointed with the other, way over to the southwest. "Time to go," he said, starting the motor. I looked and saw a small dark cloud, southwest, way out over what may have been the everglades, and I understood why.

By now, it was about midway through the outgoing tide, and bay water was running out through the cut really fast and kicking up some serious waves where the outgoing water met the ocean. Undaunted, Larry pointed the boat into the rushing waters and guided it through without incident. This was no easy task, and all the while, my heart was in my throat. Although I was a strong swimmer, I didn't want to swim home from downtown Havana.

At the dock, there were lots of folks waiting for boats to show up with fish to sell, and we were first in. We used the cast net to carry the fish to the dock where there was a cleaning station. An experienced restaurant guy, Larry was really good at filleting and skinning fish, so, while he cut and sold fillets, I pulled the boat out, removed the motor, poles, and other stuff, washed everything with the hose there on the dock, and loaded the station wagon. By the time I was done, the bait bucket and beer cooler were full of dolphin fillets, and the rest had been sold to pay for gas, more beer, and tomorrow's lunch.

That evening, we grilled Mahi-mahi and celebrated a wonderful day of fishing.

Sam Stone

# Fire from the Baseboards

**It was raining.** It wasn't one of those typical rainy seasons where it rained heavily for a few minutes and went away for an hour or so. This time, it had rained for several days, sometimes lightly and sometimes torrentially—but it never seemed to stop. I was riding "Hose Two." (When there were two engine companies rolling out of the same station, one was named "Engine" and the other was "Hose" for the simple purpose of telling one from the other.)

The fire was in the projects, a few blocks southwest of the station. They were two-story apartment buildings with poured-concrete floors and concrete-block walls. The floors of the first-floor apartments were maybe six inches above the ground.

On arrival, water in the entire neighborhood ranged from two to four inches deep and, when we entered the building, we discovered a most peculiar thing: the fire wasn't in any of the furniture or framing of the building, but was coming from behind the baseboards and under the kitchen cabinets and stoves. There were also bubbles coming up through the water surrounding the buildings, and it took very little time to ascertain that the ground surrounding and under the buildings was saturated with liquid propane gas, or "LP," as it is commonly referred to. Unlike natural gas, LP is heavier than air, and soaks into the ground. This group of about six, two-story buildings, with perhaps ten or twelve units each, had a master gas tank the length and diameter of a medium-sized submarine, with underground, galvanized pipes supplying the meters that served the apartments. From the meters, the pipes went back underground and into the walls where they were routed to individual apartments.

We made sure there wasn't anyone inside the buildings, and backed out to protect the area. Before long, the fire inspector arrived and called for a host of other inspectors from the building department, along with the federal HUD folks serving our county. Eventually, buses started rolling in to relocate all the residents of that complex.

Apparently, the underground pipes from the master tank to the buildings were not designed to run underground (and were probably installed by the low bidder). They had deteriorated badly, and had been leaking for quite some time. The gas company had been keeping the tank full without regard to how much was being consumed by the residents and how much was lost from leakage. It wasn't that big a concern until those several days of rain. Who knew how long those pipes had been leaking?

The next time we responded to a call at that complex, I noticed lots of new gas pipes running to the buildings and apartments, and concluded that the "powers-that-be" had actually followed through on the necessary repairs. That was quite an accomplishment, which was most likely due to a federal agency being involved—because the local folks didn't seem inclined to follow up on anything.

We were lucky no one had been burned or injured, and the projects were now a safer place for the residents of that area of the community.

Sam Stone

## Big Bart and the Dancer

**Big Bart Bedford was truly BIG.** He was six foot, six inches tall, and three hundred pounds—all up top—with shoulders like hams, hands like anvils, and slim from the waist down—at least for a big guy. Bart typically rode the ladder truck, and took care of all the heavy equipment. He didn't need any help setting up the generator, and he and Chuck Smiles could put that six-man, banger ladder up, just the two of them. He was a true gentle giant (at least that's what I thought), until the day he took care of "The dancer."

We responded to a domestic call over on 10th street, just off Good Bread Alley, to take care of a lady who had been beaten up pretty badly. Porter said the woman, Mary, looked like someone had danced on her face. Ernie went inside, grabbed the guy, and threw him through the front window onto the porch. Then he came out and jumped up and down on him a couple of times until Lieutenant Cosgrove pulled him off. Mary ended up in the hospital. The fellow went to the hospital that day, too—the prison ward. Mary, however, refused to press charges, and he was out the next day. She was in the hospital a week, and then went back to him. Dan Porter started calling the guy "The Dancer," and it caught on.

The next time our shift went over there was probably a year later, and that day Bart just happened to be riding the engine. Mary looked as bad as she had before, and, as soon as Ernie saw her, he started charging into the house, but Lieutenant Cosgrove and Dan Porter pulled him back. In a nice, calm voice, Bart said, "Ernie, I'll take care of this one."

After he had beaten and raped Mary, The Dancer had gone to sleep, and, while he slept, Mary stuck a carving knife in his gut. There he was, lying there on the bed, drunk, and complaining about the knife and how he "needed help." That's when Bart pulled him down on the floor, sat on his chest, and started talking calmly to him about how "it wasn't nice" to beat up on his wife that way.

Of course, with Bart's three hundred pounds on his chest, the guy couldn't breathe, and tried to push Bart off, but wasn't having any luck. All the while, Bart continued to lecture him about abusing his wife—AND, every time the guy opened an eye, Bart would spit in it. Now that might not have been so bad, except that Bart was a tobacco chewer, and, by the time it was all over, the guy's entire face was sticky brown.

While all this was happening, Ben was trying to get inside, yelling, "Let me at that bastard. I promised him I'd kick his face in next time, and I meant it!" Finally, Lieutenant Cosgrove had the policeman threaten to put Ernie in the back of the squad car until we were ready to go back to the station. Ernie fumed but behaved.

Finally, The Dancer stopped moving. That's when Bart softly counted to three hundred—more or less—and stood up. He looked down at the guy and said, "Now, remember our discussion . . . I don't want to have to come back and talk about it again." But there was no answer. The Dancer was dead.

The policeman called for the coroner, and we all swore we had seen that the guy was drunk and had fallen over, accidentally sticking himself with the knife. Unfortunately, a few months later, Mary found another guy to beat her up. This time, she went to the hospital and never came home.

Sometimes you just can't win.

# Big Jack

**Behind old Station Nine was a volleyball court, built by the guys back in the old two-platoon fire department.** Those guys stood roll call every morning, and, if you traded time with someone on the other shift, you were on duty, seventy-two consecutive hours.

The firemen on both shifts met at four o'clock every afternoon and played volleyball until sundown. They didn't rotate, and the competition was awesome. As a kid, I lived a few blocks away, and would sometimes go over to Bobby Chandler's house after dinner. His backyard faced the volleyball court, and we'd sit there and watch the guys play.

A half-dozen of them played for the YMCA. That was back when Florida State University had just gone co-ed and didn't play football. Men's volleyball was big—as in HUGE! The Miami "Y" played Florida

State for the Florida amateur volleyball championship several years running. State always won, but there were some great stories.

Billy Godwin, at about five feet six, was the set-up man. He tells about setting up Big Jack, who would jump waist high to the top of the net and look around to decide whose face he would spike the ball into. One time, during a tournament, Jack put so much energy into a spike that he blew out a hemorrhoid. Undaunted, he went into the ladies locker room, bought a half dozen feminine napkins, stuffed them in his underwear, and finished the match. Another time, he followed through so hard on a spike that he broke a guy's nose.

When I was about ten years old, the fire truck was in the neighborhood for some reason. I had a pea shooter and was shooting peas at the big shiny bell on the front bumper of the truck. Suddenly, a grizzly old guy in the driver's seat barked at me, scaring me almost to death. A little over a decade later, now a fireman myself, I swung into Station Nine to fill in for a day, and there was the same gruff guy driving Engine Nine. It was Big Jack.

All in all, both as a kid and an adult, living and working in Miami's Little River neighborhood was both educational and exciting.

Sam Stone

# Driving Chief Two

**I had been at old Station Nine long enough to be on my third District Chief.** The new guy, Ben, was amazingly prejudiced and had no use for me or my hair (long enough and thick enough for an "Afro"). My father was Jewish but, even though he had never practiced ANY religion, that didn't matter to the chief. Nor did it matter that my dad had married a "Shiksa" (a non-Jew), and I had spent my youth going to church with my maternal grandmother. The only important thing to that guy, along with six hundred, redneck firefighters was my name.

I was firstborn, after my grandfather died, and my father named me after him: Samuel. His last name was Saperstein, meaning "sapphire stone," but my father began using the last name, Stone, in his late teens, when he began working (this was before and during the Great Depression, a time when anti-Jewish sentiment was rampant among otherwise good American citizens). Many people (typically northerners) would say, "So, what's so important about the name?" I would then have to explain that, if you were a redneck, you would immediately know Sam Stone was a Jewish name.

There I was, working among a whole department of prejudiced assholes. My saving grace, however, was that I loved fighting fire, and there wasn't one of those guys who would go further into a fire than I would.

I firmly believe it was my willingness to charge into a fire without concern for my own safety that turned the chief around. After having been completely ignored by him (except when he'd tell me to get a haircut), he suddenly singled me out. "I'm transferring you to Station Thirteen to drive the engine," he announced. I was totally confused. That was his station, with Engine Thirteen rolling out the front door and Chief Two out the back. But then—and what really caught me off guard—when his driver took a day off, Ben borrowed me from the engine to drive him.

In a few months, after I had driven the chief perhaps a half-dozen times, we received an alarm for a building fire in the northwest section. There were several ways I could go, but the easiest route was straight west on Sixty-Second Street, and then north on Tenth Avenue. I headed west. I approached the green light at Seventh Avenue with the accelerator floored. This was the 70s, and the sirens were now electronic on all our trucks and equipment (much better around corners than the old style, mechanical models).

Suddenly, the siren in the chief's car began to have a physical effect on me. "The siren feels funny," I said. He asked what I meant, and I pointed at my chest and said, "It feels funny here."

"STOP!" Ben commanded (this from a man who never raised his voice). That was all I needed. I locked the brakes, skidded the station wagon sideways, and came to a stop, facing southbound in the left-turn lane of Seventh Avenue. At that very instant, Engine Six, all twenty-six thousand pounds of steel, equipment, and manpower, ran the red light and barreled through northbound, at full speed, in the southbound lane.

Our sirens had been joined in some sort of harmonic imbalance, and only my heart—which, by then was in my throat—had felt it, as I watched that truck speed through the intersection. I can still see those two—the officer and driver—staring straight ahead, seemingly without regard for the chief or me. I looked at the chief, and he simply smiled and shrugged. I cranked the wheel and drove to the fire.

From that day forward, my relationship with the chief changed forever. I was now included in conversations, and it became obvious that he was listening to me and showing respect for my ideas. I was even invited to his home for parties.

We never discussed what happened that day, or his change in attitude, but I believe there were two things going on: his respect for my aggressive fire fighting caused him to bring me to Station Thirteen in the first place; AND the incident at Sixty-Second Street cemented what was to become a lifelong friendship.

When Ben died, in order to deal with my sense of loss, I wrote a stage play about fire fighters, entitled Unlikely Hero. For a decade, the primary character's name was Ben, but I finally realized I had taken that character too far away from the real guy, so I changed the name.

To me, however, he will always be Ben—and I'll never forget him.

Thanks, Ben.

Sam Stone

# Lawrence of Oblivion

**One day, a lady called the fire department and complained about a fireman sleeping on her front lawn.** Engine Nine was dispatched. Upon arrival, there was Larry, flat on his back, out cold, with a huge bruise on the side of his head. AND, the fire hydrant, a few feet away, was running water, with a small lake forming down at the corner. Larry had been out flushing hydrants.

Now you have to understand this was south Florida, where everything's flat and the weather is good year round. Fire fighters go out on hydrant detail to either flush or paint the hydrants, riding bicycles to get there. Larry's hydrant bike was leaning against a nearby tree. The crew turned the hydrant off, revived Larry, and put him onto the front seat, loaded the hydrant bike on the tailboard of the engine, and went back to the station.

After he had rested, Larry recalled he had been bothered by a bee. He had swung the hydrant wrench at it . . . BUT . . . instead of killing the bee, he hit himself in the head. This wasn't the first time Larry had done something the captain considered beyond the line of no return, so he called the chicf and begged to have Larry moved, either to another station, shift, or whatever—as long as he was no longer at Station Nine on the B shift. The fire chief had Larry hauled downtown to his office, so he could hear, first hand, what he had to say. Well, right there in the chief's office, there just happened to be a hydrant wrench lying on a table, in plain sight. So Larry picked up the wrench and swung it, just to show the chief exactly how the incident happened—AND he did it again!

After Larry had been revived, the chief offered him the big option: Either retire—OR spend the remainder of his career working a forty-hour week, riding around on a bicycle maintaining hydrants.

Larry chose the first option, and we all breathed a lot easier.

# Geppetto

**Captain Vic was promoted to Fire Lieutenant while I was in Fire College;** he even taught a few classes and worked with us on hose evolutions (the process of laying hose in order from hydrant to the fire). This was mostly to familiarize himself with the process of riding a fire engine again, because he had been an inspector for a few years and needed retraining).

I didn't work with him after that until he made captain and came to Old Station Nine, where I was assigned. By that time, Vic, who was then approaching fifty, had some black-rimmed, granny glasses he used whenever he was doing any close-up work. We had a shop behind the station, and Vic brought in one piece of furniture at a time to restore. With his paint-stained apron, stooped posture, bow legs, and those granny glasses, he looked just like the Geppetto character in the Pinocchio story.

Needless to say, it didn't take long before that was his nickname—Geppetto.

One day, Johnny came out to the back where several of us were playing basketball and asked where Geppetto was. I immediately answered he was "in the workshop praying to his little wooden boy."

Vic was an excellent Fire Captain and an even better District Chief. We were worried when he was promoted and we lost him, but before that happened, "Geppetto" endeared himself to us in one memorable incident.

We were fighting a fire in a two-story, commercial building. There was lots of smoke and plenty of fire. Previously, we had been prohibited from opening a roof, not because of department policy (which actually encouraged such procedure, when appropriate), but because of our District Chief's "personal policy"

On this occasion, we really needed to open the roof. Captain Vic to the rescue. "Open that roof!"

he commanded. Tongue-tied Joe and I couldn't get up there fast enough.

Geppetto was no longer a storybook figure—he was our hero!

Sam Stone

# The "Dragon Wagon"
# and the First Street Bridge

**Miami's Southwest, First Street Bridge doesn't clear South River Drive by a lot**—maybe eleven feet. A couple of hundred feet before the bridge, along with huge warning signs, there's a heavy piece of steel hanging over the road at the same height as the bridge, and when a truck hits it there's a godawful noise, guaranteed to get a driver's attention.

So, we get a call to the bridge and here's this "dragon wagon," empty, on the north side. For those who don't know, a dragon wagon is a trailer for hauling large equipment. The body of the trailer is close to the ground and there's a hump where the frame comes up over the rear axles and back down again at the back with ramps for loading equipment on and off. The front of the trailer rises to about five feet in order to be carried on the truck's fifth wheel. Seen unattached, the trailer looks like the Loch Ness Monster—thus the nickname "dragon wagon."

On the other side of the bridge was a huge Caterpillar tractor on its side.

The driver was delivering the "Cat" to a job and was running late. When he ran into the dangling piece of steel, he paid no attention and kept barreling along. The Cat was mounted with the bucket forward and, according to witnesses, when the driver's cage hit the bridge, it actually rolled the Cat over backwards and then it fell over on its side.

So, Captain Jenkins called for bridge and highway inspectors, and requested police for traffic control.

The driver had called his boss, who, upon arrival, immediately called for a heavy duty wrecker. When the wrecker tried to roll the Cat back on its tracks, it only slid along the road, so they called for a second, heavy duty wrecker. Finally, one wrecker was secured to the bottom of the Cat, with the other wrecker attached to the top on the other side. In slow motion, the Cat tipped upward, and, when it became top heavy, it suddenly fell onto its tracks in an upright position—that huge thing actually seemed to bounce.

Meanwhile, the police officer wrote the driver an expensive ticket, and the boss guy was telling the driver how he, the driver, was gonna pay for the ticket and the wreckers, AND that he might keep his job, if—and only if—he promised to never drive down South River Drive again.

After the wreckers cleared, the boss guy climbed into the seat of the Cat and turned the key. Surprisingly, it cranked right up. He drove it under the bridge and onto the dragon wagon, with the track plates going clank, clank, clank along South River Drive.

During all that, the bridge inspector showed up and simply laughed. He said that bridge's framing was so heavy duty and well-designed there was no way the incident had any effect on the structure.

BUT, the highway inspector wasn't as kind. He spoke to the boss guy and got information so that the Florida State Highway Department could charge his company for repairing the damage to the road surface.

As we cleared the incident, we caught a house fire over on Southwest Fourth Street. It was one of those wood frame, craftsman style homes built during the boom days—it even had a coral rock foundation. It was such a shame to lose it, BUT . . . it was fully consumed with flames licking out the attic vent. That house was so hot you could see through it, and we had a great time putting it out. Luckily, no one was home at the time of the fire.

In all, it was an exciting and memorable afternoon.

# The Sock Sandwich

**I didn't like wearing socks in bed,** but after an hour in my firefighting boots, my feet would complain, so I started carrying a fresh pair of socks in the back pocket of my bunker pants. After a fire is knocked down, and overhaul begins, there's typically time to take a minute to put your socks on. The problem was that the pocket wasn't waterproof, and my socks would get wet.

Now, this was the seventies, and grocery stores were still using paper bags. So, one day, when I emptied a plastic bread bag, I was inspired to use it to protect my socks.

The next time we put out a fire, and we had started overhaul, my feet started to chafe. I went outside, and, right there in front, was a police car. I sat on the hood, kicked off my boots, and pulled the plastic sock bag from my back pocket. The policeman looked quizzically at the package. I suddenly realized it looked sort of like a sandwich wrapped in the bread bag . . . so . . . I held it out to him and said, "Hungry?" He rolled his eyes and looked away.

Then, I opened the bag, took out my socks and put them on.

I'll never forget the look on that police officer's face. It was priceless!

# The Rooming House Fire

**I was trading time with a Fire Fighter on another shift at Station Two,** when an alarm came in for a building fire in the northwest section. This was a typical two-story rooming house with a single interior stairway, one restroom on each floor, and eight or ten individual rooms per floor. The building was filled with smoke. Luckily all the residents were already out.

The fire was in a front room on the ground floor, and had gotten into the wall. The Captain assigned another Fire Fighter and me to, "Pull the siding off the building." We grabbed a pike pole from Ladder Two and rushed to the side of the building where fire was coming out of the window. We shoved the pike section of the pole between layers of siding, up near the roof, and rotated it so the hook was toward the wall—and we pulled. Surprisingly, a full twenty-foot length of siding came loose from the building, floated down, and landed flat on the ground next to the building.

This was a "boom-time" building, certainly constructed before 1920, possibly around the turn of the century, and not long after the railroad came to Miami. These types of buildings wcrc cheaply made, and built for the many black singles and couples, who were the laborers found in all areas of town. There was no insulation in the walls, or even sub-siding, so behind the section of siding we had removed, there was only the stud wall, which made it easier to pull off more siding. We had only to hook onto the top of the next lowest piece of lumber—and pull.

The other guy on the pike pole was a probationary Fire Fighter, recently out of the fire college. He was easy to recognize—about six feet four (maybe more) and about two-fifty, all up top. This guy had arms like power poles, a wasp waist, and looked like he could move mountains. In almost no time, I realized I was only hanging onto the pole, while he pulled section after section of siding off the building, using me as ballast. He would lift the pole (with my feet coming off the ground), and the next time my feet touched down, another section of siding was falling to the ground. It took very little time to get down to the part of the wall that was on fire, and, once exposed, the fire was extinguished easily.

That young man rapidly rose through the ranks, and eventually became our Fire Chief. He was a capable and respected leader, at a time when we needed such a person in charge.

As for me? Well, I continued to be the "captain's hemorrhoid" for the remainder of my career.

# Sam Stone

# Sky King

**A few years ago, when I attended the annual Fire Fighters reunion in Otto, North Carolina,** most of the regulars were there. The previous two years it had rained, and the reunion was held in the meeting hall owned by the Otto Fire Department (founded by retired District Chief Ben Durfey). This year, however, it was clear and dry, and we were back in Ronnie Hardegree's back yard—yeah, that beautiful green space that starts next to the garage and gently glides downhill to the pond with the gazebo in the middle (kinda like an amphitheater with plenty of room for all those folks).

There were two hundred and fifteen people in attendance—nearly a hundred fewer than in the previous several years. You could tell it, too—there was way too much green space between the tables. Tongue-Tied Joe was missing, along with the rest of the crowd from Tallahassee. I always liked talking to Joe. He spoke as if he were tongue-tied but he wasn't—who knew why.

At one point, I turned around and there was one of the few guys I had wished never to see again. He had been the captain at Station Ninc on thc "B" shift, since before "The Flood," and he was still there when I swung in with nearly ten years on the job. I'd heard all the stories about him, and I thought about the decision for quite some time, before volunteering to go there. However, I had grown up just a half-mile from that station—over by the elementary school—and knew the entire territory better than most of the guys in the station. Hell, I can even remember when they built that huge water tower over by the tracks. At the time, it was the biggest one in all of south Florida.

Did I mention that the most common thing about good Fire Fighters is that they're territory freaks? They remember every landmark; know where all the businesses are; they don't have to be told where the fire hydrants are (because they've committed them all to memory); and know which direction the lights are staggered.

The day I walked into Station Nine, personnel folder in hand, Leonard took one look at my folder and exclaimed he'd never seen one that thick. Hell, mine was nowhere near as thick as Roger's or Bill's, and Chucky's was so thick Lieutenant Turner had to split it into two folders—and Chucky only had fifteen years on the job. Based upon that information alone, I assumed something I already knew: There was a leadership problem at Station Nine that extended far beyond the stories I'd heard.

The captain acted like he was the king of the station and treated the Fire Fighters as if their only purpose in life was to be there for him to insult. Of course, the only reason he could be like that was because the District Chief, one of the most inept leaders on the face of the earth, allowed it.

Within two days of my assignment to Station Nine, I had this guy pegged. He had a litany of abuses he subjected the guys to every day on duty, beginning with morning school. He had unkind one-liners and pet names for every member of the crew, and, immediately, I came to the conclusion that I wasn't going to let him treat me that way. My dad was Jewish, and, although I was only half-

Jewish and was raised in the church, I was the closest thing to a "Jew Boy" among six hundred, "redneck" Fire Fighters.

The guys at old Station Three called me "Jew Boy" during my first year on the job, but, from them, it was just friendly banter, so I had fun with it. AND, with a name like mine, there was no way of avoiding the Jewish thing, anyway, so I just embraced it. Sometimes, it took me quite a while to separate those who used that expression out of friendliness from those bastards who were downright prejudiced, but, with the captain at Station Nine, it took less than a heartbeat.

Lucky for him, he was smart enough to never call me that name.

You have to understand the demographics of those guys to truly grasp the situation. At six feet tall and two hundred pounds, I was one of the smallest guy on the crew. HOWEVER, it took me very little time to establish a reputation as one of the most aggressive Fire Fighters in that end of town—with the exception of Doug. "Johnny Crooked-Jaw" once said he was certain that Doug and I would attack the fires of hell with a leaky garden hose, while all the time fighting for the nozzle. I believe it was Archimedes who said he could move the world if he had a long enough lever. Hell, I knew in my heart that I was that lever. With a thirty-two inch waist and shoulders like hams, I moved those larger guys around like matchsticks. (It's a shame I don't look much like that today.)

One guy, not in any way a friend, once called me, "Jew Boy." I told him, "Only my friends call me Jew Boy, you prejudiced fuck—and you can be goddamned sure you ain't one of them!" He just stood there, staring at me in disbelief. The silence in that room, containing fifteen giants and a huge spotted dog, was deafening. "Do we understand each other, Ass Hole?" I asked. He just nodded, unmoving. Somehow I managed to speak very quietly and said, "Next time I promise you . . . a minimum of three broken bones, and you'll never walk or talk right again."

Johnnie Crooked Jaw looked at me, smiled, and winked. No one ever said anything about that morning.

Lenny continued to complain about how his personnel folder only had a few pages, while mine was as thick as it was. One afternoon, when I was on watch, and only the two of us were in the office, we got out our folders and compared them. It took seconds to realize that the captain hadn't been doing his job when it came to the "anecdotal record" part of the crew's folders. Lenny had been on the job two years longer than I had, but only his folder had only two pages of notes, while mine contained probably a page for every year. I also noticed there were no entries in my record since I had been assigned there, even though we had fought several serious fires and dealt with a good number of interesting incidents, including the time I lassoed the burning boat in the middle of the Little River Canal. I swore to correct that problem.

The next fire was a good sized one, and we did everything right. After we returned to the station and were loading hose and cleaning the equipment, the captain said something like, "Helluva job, guys. That was a great stop." I knew I had him, and said, "Captain, you said it, now put it in my record."

I was surprised when the entire crew, as if they had rehearsed it, said, in unison, "Yeah, me too!"

From then on, almost on a daily basis, and without making it obvious, I taught those guys, through example, how to make that bastard do his job. By the time he finally transferred out of our lives, every man in the station had his number.

Mickey had a construction business on his day off, and every third time the station phone rang it was for him. The captain had a habit of hollering, "Mickey's Construction!" whenever the phone rang— just another example of his unkindness, but we brought that to an end also.

The captain bought a small plane. He and his buddies would fly to Naples or Orlando just for lunch, and, with aviation gas at only forty-five cents a gallon, it wasn't all that expensive. It didn't take long before his fellow flyboys were calling on a regular basis to plan for the following day's flight.

I filled in for Lenny as station chef whenever he was off. It had long been the habit for the cook to answer the phone during meals. One lunch, the phone rang, and, as I ran to the office, I could hear that bum saying, "Mickey's Construction!"

Turned out it was one of the flyboys, and, after setting the phone down, I hollered, "Sky King!" You could hear the laughter and comments from the dining room all the way across the street. I'm sure the guy on the phone heard it too, and, within a few days, the flyboys were asking for Sky King when they called.

Eventually, the captain made one of the greatest management blunders of his career. At morning school, he announced that we weren't to use that expression any longer. My union negotiator training took over, and I immediately responded to the hypocrisy of the statement and asked if that was going to apply equally to all the mean-spirited things he constantly said about the rest of the guys in the room. Caught off guard, he began to stammer without really saying anything, so I continued, "I guess it's going to be 'Sky King' until you show some leadership in that area, right?"

By then, the guys were learning to use his hypocrisy against him, and they all jumped "in his garbage" with both feet. Over the next month or so, we watched his slow transformation, as the unkind comments ground to a halt. During that time, our horse's ass of a district chief was transferred to the south end of town. The new chief had excellent management skills, and, somehow, was able to get our guy transferred downtown and out of our lives.

Over the next several years at Station Nine, we helped four captains study and prepare for the test for District Chief. They were all among the best captains and district chiefs I'd ever worked with, and we all took credit for helping to make a lot of it happen.

Back to the reunion. Standing there on Ronnie's deck, I just held out my hand and said, "Hello, how're you doing?" My enthusiasm caught him off guard. He just stammered, and his handshake was like a wet rag. I knew I had his number. Walking away, I hacked loudly and spit on my hand, wiping it clean with my handkerchief (knowing all the while that bastard was watching) before kissing Gene and Big Lenny hello. But that's another story, one about trust, respect and friendship—the kind that comes from placing your life in another man's hands and living to tell about it, decades later.

That reunion was all about a bunch of white-haired old guys with bad knees telling stories about their youth. I patiently listened to, and laughed at, their stories for the umpteenth time each, and even told a few of my own—AND every time I saw that bastard looking my way, I gave him a look of contempt and spit.

Next year, he didn't show.

# Mirror, Mirror

**Charlie "Hammerhand," known to the rest of the world as Charles Hammond, had huge forearms** that went from his elbows to his hands with no discernible constriction where most folks have a wrist. As a result, he had trouble keeping a wristwatch in place. He also didn't like anything constricting, such as an expansion watchband. He solved the problem by wearing a pocket watch in a leather holder, attached to his belt.

With just a little over a year on the job, I was the "rookie" on Engine Three's tailboard, along with Charlie and Dan. Lieutenant Cosgrove rode in the truck's right front seat, and Big Joe was the driver.

Charlie was a gutsy fire fighter, who could really take the heat, one of those guys who would attack the fires of hell with a garden hose. More often than I'd care to admit, I swore I was never again going to follow him into a fire, but I knew I didn't really mean it. (Going all the way into the seat of a fire and then opening the nozzle can be amazingly rewarding.)

One afternoon, we responded to a fire in a laundry about two blocks from the station. On arrival, we could see bright flames through the front display window, with black smoke billowing out of every opening, and we knew the fire had totally engulfed the building. The front door was wide open, and Big Joe stopped the truck with the tailboard just beyond it. I was on the side of the tailboard nearest the fire, and pulled the jump line, a two-hundred foot length of inch-and-a-half hose, pre-connected to Engine Three's pump. Charlie cleared the compartment and stretched out the line, as Big Joe ran up pressure and opened the valve to the line.

This was at a point before we were issued self-contained (air) breathing apparatus, so I didn't have to take time to go back to the truck and put one on. We did have MSA filters mounted in pockets, sewn into the back of our bunker coats, with hoses over our shoulders to masks dangling at the end. Holding the nozzle between my knees, I put my mask on and moved into the building.

It was the early 60s, and polyester hadn't become popular yet, so most of the flammable construction materials and contents of buildings were either wood, cotton, or some other natural fiber. Within a year or so, two things would happen: first, synthetic materials became a big thing, not only in clothing, but building materials as well, and fire fighting became infinitely more hazardous; second, our department carried self-contained breathing equipment (air packs) for every member of the crew on all trucks, making fire fighting infinitely safer. Until that time, most inner city firefighters didn't live more than five years after retirement. Now, they live decades longer—due mostly to self-contained breathing apparatus.

Opening the nozzle in a wide, fog pattern, I pushed the fire through the door and into the building ahead of me. The hose was easy to maneuver, and I knew Charlie was behind me pulling it along.

The laundry had two sections. The front area, facing the street, had a counter where customers dropped off clothing for washing or dry cleaning. An overhead trolley traveled from the front section to the back with clothes hanging from it.

After knocking down most of the fire in the front section, there was a still a large amount of flames over the front counter. I was throwing huge quantities of water at it with no success. The heat was reaching a point that was nearly unbearable, and I still had no idea why I couldn't put out the fire.

Finally, Charlie spun me around to face the street, and there, above the display window, was a shelf, loaded with supplies and fully engulfed by the fire. Apparently, there was a mirror above the counter that was reflecting an image of the actual fire, and all I had been doing was washing the mirror clean. (Later on, we had a good laugh about that one.)

After knocking down that part of the fire, we moved into the back room. Upon its arrival, Engine Fifteen hand-dragged a supply line to Engine Three, assuring that we wouldn't run out of water. Then, they opened the back door and were fighting fire from that direction, using a hose off their truck. Of course the smoke was so thick we didn't know that until we met them in the middle.

Suddenly, Charlie was screaming and pulling his bunker coat off. I didn't know what was happening, but I kept him cool with water from the nozzle. When he had the coat completely off, he pulled the filter out of the pocket in the back of his coat, and it was so hot it was steaming. Those filters had some sort of material in them that worked to convert carbon monoxide into something harmless—maybe carbon dioxide—but I didn't really don't know what. When they got overloaded with carbon monoxide, they heated up quickly. Charlie put the coat back on, and we got back to the business of fighting the fire. After that, he stayed low in the cooler, cleaner air and breathed through his nose.

This was long before the guys on the task force team came up with the idea of a smoke chute, and there weren't many openings in that place. It seemed like it was going to take forever to ventilate the smoke and heat, until Ladder Four cut a "four-by-four" in the roof, and stuck a fan in the opening. The smoke cleared a lot faster after that.

When we had the fire out, we discovered we had hundreds of wire hangers hooked on the hoses. It took an hour or more to untangle the mess.

The Fire Inspector came by the station later and told us the fire had started in a clothes dryer, due to a worn part that became overheated. This was a large, popular laundry, and I sometimes wonder how many families' laundry went up in smoke that day. I sure hope the laundry's insurance was paid up.

After the fire, we rolled up the wet hose, loaded it on the tailboard, and returned to the station, where we reloaded hose and cleaned the truck. When Charlie took his bunker coat off, we discovered a large blister on his back. While Dan and I loaded dry hose, Big Joe took Charlie out back of the station and cut a leaf from a huge aloe plant. He rubbed the liquid from the plant onto the blister on Charlie's back. For the remainder of our shift, the entire crew took turns rubbing aloe onto Charlie's back every hour or so.

The next day on duty, Charlie reported it had already scabbed over.

I'm still embarrassed when I think about washing the mirror clean that was reflecting the fire over my shoulder. I also think about what a terrific crew we had on old Engine Three.

Sam Stone

# Mister Clean

**One fellow at the station was amazingly clean.**
Even after a fire, his bunker gear was sparkling white, while mine always looked like I had been rolling around in the ashes. I was riding the engine company, and this guy was on the ladder, so I never had much opportunity to watch him at a fire, but he always seemed to be busy.

Eventually, I asked "Tongue-Tied Joe" about it, and he simply said, "The guy never goes in the fire. Oh, yeah, he stays busy, but that's part of the deal. He plays with the generator and such, so the captain won't send him inside to do anything."

The guy was also extremely neat, spending what seemed like hours making sure the folds on the back of his shirts were perfect.

Finally, one day, Jimmy T told me to take "Mister Clean" on the side and tell him the windshield on his new truck was warped. That would have been curious, as the guy had just recently traded up from a '51 Chevrolet to a '62 model (I believe this may have been the last year of Chevy's wrap-around windshield). Out in the parking lot, I took a look and could casily see that within the area where the windshield wrapped around, things got a little distorted. This wouldn't have bothered me even the slightest, but I could understand how this guy would have a fit over it being less than perfect.

S-o-o-o-o, I waited until he and I were in the lobby alone, and quietly said, "Did you know that your truck windshield is warped?"

What followed was nearly a half-hour litany of events that had him discovering the windshield was warped, and him going to a glass shop to have it replaced. Well, the replacement windshield was also warped, so he went back to the glass shop, which put in another one. Eventually, the glass guy ended up putting Mister Clean's original glass back in and telling him they all were warped and that's why GM stopped doing wrap-around windshields. (I'm sure the glass guy had no idea what he was getting into when he took on the job of replacing Mister Clean's windshield, but probably wished they'd never met.)

Over the next few days, Jimmy T made sure everyone on our shift and at least a few guys on the other shifts mentioned the warped windshield to Mister Clean, AND by the time it was all over—and as soon as he could afford to—he traded that truck in for another.

The ladder truck in our station was a straight truck with a sixty-five foot, aerial ladder. Eventually, however, when the department bought one of those one hundred fifty foot towers for downtown, we inherited Station One's hundred-foot senior aerial. It was the kind that bent in the middle, and had a driver at each end.

I was next up for driver, but the captain promoted Mister Clean to that position, instead. I didn't want to have a confrontation while on duty, so I went by the captain's house the next day and asked why I was passed over. His response was simple. He was very much aware that Mister Clean was afraid of fire, and there was no way that guy would ever be found inside a fire. But, the guy was meticulously clean, so the best way the captain could use this guy to his full capability was to let him spend every morning cleaning and caring for the ladder truck. At the time, I argued against the captain's decision, but eventually, I came to the conclusion he was right.

As a result, Laddcr Nine was the absolute cleanest truck in town. And, besides, if I had been given the job driving the ladder, and we responded to an exciting fire, I would have eaten my heart out watching the engine guys charging inside, while I was busy on the outside setting up the generator and fans. The extra five percent pay I would have derived from driving wouldn't have made up for the excitement of going all the way inside a fire and spraying the clear stuff on the red stuff—at least not for a cardiac kid like me.

Drive on, Mister Clean. Drive on.

# The Mouse Trap Restaurant Fire

**There I was, out in front of Fire Station Nine, leaning back in that metal office chair** with my feet on the flagpole. This was nothing unusual except for the fact that it was two o'clock in the morning and I was wide awake. There was a stiff breeze coming in from the east and I could smell the bay (or ocean—whichever) and I was thinking about going shrimping the following night. I remember reminding myself to check the sports section for the tides.

Without warning, smoke began to roll through the station and down the street. It was dark and thick and could barely get off the ground—and smelled like a lot more than just wood. Instantly on my feet, I grabbed the chair and sprinted the twenty feet to the front door. I left the chair in the Captain's office, as I raced through to the watch desk, all the time wondering what to do first: call the alarm office, or ring the station bell.

The question was answered with a single ding of the station bell, indicating the alarm office was energizing our bell line. I stepped out of my shoes, turned on the house lights and the station's radio speakers, stepped into my turnout boots, and pulled the suspenders over my shoulders, while preparing to write the assignment on the pad. It took forever (probably three or four seconds in real time) for the radio to begin its attention-getting squeal, and I knew we were in for a building assignment. (It takes longer for them to prepare to announce building assignments, because they have to energize the bell lines for several stations.)

The fire was on Biscayne Boulevard, located in no-man's land—you know, that area surrounded by the "China Walls," south of the Little River canal, and east of the tracks. The old story that says, "You can't get there from here," is true about that area, and, in order to cross the tracks, you either go north to Seventy-Ninth Street or south to Sixty-Second.

I finished writing the assignment, noticing that Engine Twelve was the second engine assigned, and handed the page and carbon to the officers, as they passed through. Racing to Engine Nine, I donned my helmet and coat, hopped into the jump-seat, and prayed, "Dear God, please make him turn right at Fourth Court." Lieutenant Wally had just been promoted to captain and there was a brand new lieutenant and an even newer driver in the front seat. Neither knew the territory, and they were up there all alone.

After the driver had been assigned, I had tried to advise him, several times, to be careful of the Boulevard. There are very few hydrants in the section between Sixty-Second and Seventy-Ninth Streets, and the few that are there have very little water. The Boulevard main is old and small, and there's too much demand. Some old guy flushes his toilet over by the bay and Engine Nine sucks the hydrant dry.

We passed Fourth Court, and my heart sank as we went to the Boulevard and turned right. A block from the fire, I knew it was The Mouse Trap, a large restaurant and night spot for those folks who wanted to be seen around town. It had a marquee out front, large enough for two cars to pass through, side-by-side, and the flames coming through the wide open, double doors ran the length of the marquee and punched a hole in the clouds.

What to do? I didn't worry about conserving water. I pulled the two and a half-inch, pre-connect line and opened the nozzle into the front doors, filling the opening with a fog pattern and one hundred fifty-plus gallons of water a minute.

I actually darkened the entire entrance lobby before I heard the Engine Nine's motor winding up, and knew it was running away from the water. I shut down the nozzle knowing three things: one, I'd used up all the water in Engine Nine's five hundred gallon tank; two, we hadn't received a supply line; and, three, the nearest hydrant was on the corner of Fifth Avenue—a tenth of a mile west and too far to hand drag a supply line.

Engine Thirteen, our nearest neighbor, wasn't responding. They were holding down Station Two, because there was a fire downtown, and they weren't going to bring us our usual timely supply line. Finally, after what seemed an eternity, Engine Twelve, coming from way out west, brought us water.

It seemed like hours before we finally got water on the fire again (maybe five to eight minutes in real time) but, by then, the fire had grown and this time it took two lines abreast to darken the door and lobby.  The dining room of the restaurant was even worse, because it was larger and had more to burn.

After the fire was knocked down and we got some lights and fans working, we found seven plastic, five-gallon jugs of gasoline on tabletops—all with the tops burned off.

Thankfully, as gasoline burns, the evaporation process cools the remainder of the liquid below the flame.  That kept the containers from burning and spilling their entire contents, making the fire even hotter (there was already enough of that going on.)  I personally carried out three of the containers.  We lined them up along the curb, and, after the inspector took photos and samples, one of the neighbors came up with a gas can, a long handled dipper, and a funnel.  It was a great opportunity for public relations, and we had a ball taking care of the neighbors.

Several years later, the police nabbed a mobster from New York for something really serious, and, during interrogation, he confessed to setting our fire. The owner had refused to pay "protection," and they had burned her out of business. This guy was just another soldier doing his job. Some soldier. You'd think we were caught in a war zone.

Luckily, not one of the jugs of gasoline was knocked off a table during the firefighting process. If that had happened, we could have lost a couple of Fire Fighters in there . . . and . . . guess who would have been right behind the nozzle?

Thankfully, The Mouse Trap turned out to be just another exciting fire—and not the disaster it could have been.

# The Orange Bowl Parade
# and the Battery Guy

**The Orange Bowl Parade and Orange Bowl Game had both been around probably half a century,** maybe longer, when Ernie Siler came up with the name, "King Orange Jubilee." As the Director of the City of Miami's Parks Department, he was the guy who seized upon the idea of corporate-sponsored theme floats, a block long. From that point forward, hometown-style, parade entries were no longer allowed in the "big parade." When the job of running the annual festival got too big, Ernie retired from the city and went full time King Orange.

The festival was, and still is, a weeklong "thing," with major and minor activities around South Florida, including: boat races; water ski shows; gala country club events; fishing tournaments; sporting events; two parades; and the big game itself. This "thing" is HUGE with a capital "H," and the King Orange Parade played a major role in making it so.

Then there was this guy who had a battery business. Come the big parade, he'd drive his truck downtown to the float staging area, and spend the entire day making sure everyone's engines and generators were started and working properly—and he never charged for this service. After the parade was over, and well behind the actual parade, but before they opened the street to vehicular traffic, he would drive his battery truck along the parade route and go home. Sometimes, the local television station showed him in the background while the announcers closed the program.

Finally, one year, some minor parade official met the battery guy at the entrance to the lot and informed him that if he wished to drive his truck along the parade route he must pay for the privilege.

The battery guy didn't say a word. He just turned his truck around and left. He never returned, and there was plenty of confusion that first year. After that, the committee had to pay quite a bit to keep someone around to perform the service they previously received for nothing, other than looking the other way while the battery guy rolled along the parade route.

Over the years, I felt privileged to have been invited to attend a few Orange Bowl Committee meetings. My float had won the Junior Orange Bowl Parade's amateur division one year, and was reserve champion another (perhaps they felt I made a meaningful contribution). Mostly, I listened and watched. Many members of the committee were owners or directors of large businesses there in town. There were also folks from the artistic, social, and athletic communities, who made sure there were enough activities all week to keep VIPs and other visitors occupied.

So, why would the committee bother itself with something as miniscule and unimportant as that battery truck?

It's entirely possible that not one of the committee members even knew about the battery guy; it's easy to assume they had no idea what was going on at the lot where all the floats collected. Why should they? They had employees and volunteers to do that.

Perhaps the weasel who drove the battery guy off was acting on his own, trying to prove how important he was by bringing in another fifty dollars, and, perhaps, earning himself a chance to move up in the organization. If so, I got the feeling it didn't work out as well as he'd planned.

We folks who grew up in South Florida, especially in the fifties, loved the parade. Most of us sat in our living rooms and watched it on television, while others made it a point to go downtown and watch it in person.

In 2002, the Orange Bowl Committee, in its great wisdom, decided the parade was too much of a financial burden, and shut it down. The parade typically cost a million dollars to produce, and the income it generated was only eight hundred thousand, so their decision to save two hundred thousand seemed to be reasonably sound. But . . . what the committee didn't consider were the millions of dollars spent locally at hotels, in restaurants, on entertainment, transportation, and a host of other areas by marching bands, members of corporations sponsoring floats, the local laborers, who built the floats, and folks from out of town, who came to watch or participate in the parade.

Perhaps as much as a half million dollars, maybe more, was spent on parade day, at restaurants and street vendors, by the folks who attended the parade. Then there were the tourists who went to Miami's "Little Havana" by the thousands to enjoy food, entertainment, and Miami's unique Cuban atmosphere. Because there was no parade, however, many no longer came to spend their money. It's estimated that the South Florida community has lost ten million dollars in revenue—maybe a lot more—since the parade was canceled.

I sometimes wonder how much, or how little, research goes into making that kind of decision. Probably the same amount of research that went into asking the battery guy to pay for driving his truck down the parade route on his way home.

A couple of pretty costly decisions, if you ask me.

Sam Stone

# The Kite Caper

**My next door neighbors were from Peru, and they had a passel of kids.** One of them, a boy, was in his early teens and spent considerable time playing with my kids. One day, we were talking about kites, and I learned that folks from his country build and fly lots of kites—and he grew up in kite country.

Under his direction, we built a kite on my kitchen table and took it over to the park to fly it. Wow! as soon as I let it go, it soared directly overhead and stayed there motionless. It had an open triangle built into the length of the center that kept it faced, unmoving, into the wind. It was terrific.

A week or so later, I took some materials to the fire station and built another one, only it was a lot bigger—about six feet wide and eight feet long. I worked on it all afternoon, putting up with lots of comments and suggestions from the guys (all in good humor).

After dinner, Lieutenant Bill and Captain Jenkins went to a district meeting. The last thing Lieutenant Bill said before leaving was, "Don't fly the kite!"

Well, soon as they were gone, Tongue Tied Joe and Johnny Crooked Jaw started pushing me to fly the darned thing, saying that if I didn't, they would. Truth is, I should have let them do it.

I had brought some lightweight nylon string with me, the same string I had used for the smaller kite the kids and I had made. We took the kite outside and hooked it up. It went a hundred feet or so overhead, and, when I tried to hold it back, the string broke. Thankfully, the wind was out of the west, so I got on the hydrant bike, rode a couple of blocks away, and chased it down. Bringing it back, I held the string a couple of feet below the kite and pedaled the bike with the kite flying along with me.

When I returned, we doubled the string and flew it again, and, just like before, it went straight up a few hundred feet and stayed there facing the wind without moving.

We hadn't paid attention to the time, and hadn't been watching the street, so when a car pulled into the parking lot, my heart sank. As he exited the car, the only thing Lieutenant Bill said was, "Get that thing out of the sky!" He marched straight into the station, with Joe and Johnny close on his heels, while Doug and I brought the kite down and lashed it to my truck.

The guys weren't able to convince Lieutenant Bill to hold off, and he wrote an entry in my anecdotal record stating I had violated a direct order. (I still have my folder, several decades after retirement, and the entry is still there.)

The following day, Saturday, the power boat squadron had a cookout at the firefighters clubhouse. Billy Lee loaned me his heavy duty reel, a homemade thing about a foot in diameter he used when trolling for sharks, and bolted to a stick maybe three feet long. I had picked up some stronger line, and we got the kite up to what felt like a thousand feet—maybe more. Ben swore it was a half mile in the sky. We drove a spike into the ground and secured the stick to it, so we didn't have to hold it. The kids were all sending letters up the string, addressed to "The Man In The Moon."

Meanwhile, the wind, which had started the afternoon coming off the ocean, eventually swung around to the west. The clubhouse was under the airport's landing pattern, and, for some reason, it seemed the planes were coming in a little higher than normal. All of a sudden, a sedan with no markings, but bearing a flashing yellow light on its top, came screaming into the parking lot, and a huge guy "unfolded" out of it. It was a full-size sedan, but the guy was so large he made it look like a toy, kind of like the clown car at the circus. The guy was wearing a uniform I'd never seen before and it was evident—because of the badge on his chest, patches on his sleeves, and the enormous gun on his hip—that he was serious. The guy was some sort of federal officer, security person, or someone working for the FAA at the airport, and he was on a mission.

He pulled a large folding knife that looked a lot like a machete out of a pouch on his belt, opened it, and spoke very calmly, saying, "You're in the flight path for incoming planes. Either you bring that thing down, or I cut the string."

My heart was in my throat. All I could think about was the kite being sucked into a jet engine and me spending the rest of my life in some federal prison.

By now, the wind had picked up and the kite was difficult to bring down. Ben kept the guy engaged in conversation, while Billy Lee and Crazy Larry walked hand-over-hand down the string and pulled it back toward me, while I cranked the wheel. All the while, the guy was screaming, "It's taking too long!"

Finally, when the kite was on the ground, the guy gave us a final warning and squeezed himself back into the sedan and disappeared. I finally breathed easier.

By then, I'd had enough problems with the kite, so I gave it to Billy Lee, who took it to the power squadron's clubhouse out in Stiltsville, in south Biscayne Bay. He said they let the string completely out, with a twenty-foot-long tail attached to the kite, and it flew great—until the rain came.

I didn't make another kite for about ten years. Got in trouble with that one, too—but that's another story.

# The Overseas Railroad

**Over the summer of my probationary year as a Fire Fighter, I was assigned to old Station Four.** That's where I met Captain Ray Green.

The station was located in an older neighborhood, separated from downtown by the Miami River. It had condos along the bay, a few gated estates. and a large, middle-class section split in half by Henry Flagler's railroad.

This was the least active fire station on the face of the earth. Sometimes, they would go nearly a month without an alarm, and I would have gone crazy were it not for Captain Green. He was a wonderful storyteller, along with being a true gentleman and a born leader of men.

The entire crew, except for me, were all married men. From sundown until about 10 PM, they'd walk up and down the sidewalk discussing, of all things, worldly affairs, the upcoming elections, and marital problems. With me being twenty-one years of age and having more muscles than common sense, that kind of talk just wasn't enough to capture my attention. There were no fires to fight; no middle-aged women with hypertension to send to the hospital; and no pool table on which I could hone my talents—in short, there was nothing for me to do!

One day, Captain Green was sitting on a lawn chair in front of the station, and I sat down next to him and said something about not having the patience to wait for "the next alarm that may never happen."

He laughed and said, "I used to be like you."

Yeah, sure, I thought.

Then, aloud, I said, "So . . . how'd you get over it?"

"W-e-l-l-l-l, there was this hurricane . . ."

The rest of the evening, he told me about the BIG hurricane. It was an event I had heard of all my life, but I never quite understood what truly happened to South Florida until that day.

Ray spoke about homes in the Florida Keys being blown completely away; century-old trees that were uprooted; boats and ships that either sunk or were either washed or blown onshore; and, finally, he told me the story of the overseas railroad.

You see, when Henry Flagler brought his railroad to Miami in the late 1800s, the place began to boom like nobody's business. His Royal Palm Hotel, a rambling, four-story wood structure that covered several acres, was on the north side of the mouth of the Miami River, an area now known as Bayfront Park. It had huge wooden verandas for the guests to stroll, or to sit on and enjoy the warm breeze coming in off the bay. (Unfortunately, it was demolished in 1930, after being declared a fire hazard.)

By the summer of 1935, Mr. Flagler's "Overseas Railroad" had been running all the way to Key West for twenty-three years, bridging the long spans between the islands with wonderfully constructed pilings and bulwarks. Hundreds of laborers, mostly African Americans, kept the track rails and buildings in excellent repair. Knowing the hurricane was coming, but wanting to get as much labor for its money as possible, the railroad waited until the last minute to evacuate the laborers. It turned out they waited at least a half day too long, because the train was washed off the tracks by a windblown wave.

Ray, a young fireman at the time, was one of many laborers recruited to help clean up the Keys. He spoke of wading among the mangroves to drag bloated bodies ashore, and how fishing boats had been employed to net bodies in the ocean and bringing them in. They stacked the corpses among railroad ties, doused them with oil, and burned them to reduce the potential for illness among the survivors.

Grown men would step back from the chore of stacking and burning, and break into loud wailing and heaving sobs, shedding gallons of tears, only to wipe their nose on their sleeve and go back to work.

The train never ran to the Florida Keys again, and the Flagler roadbed, including the pilings and supports that crossed the waterways, was sold to the state of Florida. Eventually, they paved a road all the way to Key West, and named it "The Overseas

Highway"—eventually also known as U.S. Highway Number One.

Captain Ray had a full and rewarding career, retiring not long after the summer I spent at Station Four. He enjoyed many years of comfortable retirement before his passing.

I think of him regularly with fondness.

Goodbye old friend.

Sam Stone

# The Tiddlywink
# and the Seeing-Eye Dog

**There are times when an eighty-pound manhole cover behaves like a tiddlywink.** Believe me, when that happens, you can either hang onto your ass—or kiss it goodbye. (Okay, I won't talk about the one that Ladder Two sent skittering across Miami Avenue—right at some poor guy's knees. That story's too gruesome for ordinary folks to handle.)

"Harry The Blind Guy" could typically be found walking around downtown Miami, and occasionally you'd see him at the far north end of Goodbread Alley—or way out on West Flagler Street. After hours, almost every night, you could also find him at Club Fifteen, sitting in the loveseat next to the combo playing blues.

Harry was big and black, and had a white Labrador retriever, seeing-eye dog named Jet. If you were obtuse enough to mention that Harry was black and the dog was white, he'd ask, "What's white and black?"

He had a wonderful memory for voices. After the second time you introduced yourself, all you had to say was, "Hi, Harry," and he'd respond with, "Hello, Sam. What's the latest?" He also knew the complete history of Miami, and had a way of telling stories that left you wanting more.

Harry was always impeccably dressed, and quite often attached to a beautiful woman with huge breasts. Where he found the women, who knew, but rarely did I see him with the same woman twice. There's a possibility the local pimps and dealers kept him supplied, in return for certain activities such as "deliveries." I once asked him why he needed Jet, when he always had a woman to lead him around. He regarded me in such a manner that I swore he could see through me, and said, "Sam, these women can't even find their way home, much less guide me to Moe's Barber Shop."

If you said hello to Harry at Club Fifteen, he'd introduce you to the woman sitting with him, by her first name only, and say, "Show Sam your stuff, honey." Right there, in front of the entire crowd, the girl would pull up her blouse and show herself off, shaking her chest with pride.

One Friday afternoon, Roger and I went to the laundry at Southwest Two and Flagler to pick up our uniforms. Harry and Jet were on Flagler Street, heading west. I asked Harry why he and Jet were alone. He said, "When I want to hold a meaningful conversation, it's just Jet and me." I laughed and went inside to retrieve my starched shirts.

On the way out of the laundry, crossing the street, shirts in hand, I looked east and noticed a ball of fire at Miami Avenue, as a manhole cover blew about ten feet in the air, followed by another one, even closer, going off under a car. As manhole covers continued to blow, one at a time, in rapid succession toward me, I only had time to make sure I wasn't standing on one. After the one to my right went off, I looked to the left in time to see the next one blow right under Jet, who, luckily, had all four feet planted on the cover. In a flash, he went from zero altitude to shoulder-high elevation.

Lucky for Jet, the manhole cover didn't flip over. It came down flat, but Jet kept jumping up and down making some of the most unusual noises, which sounded nothing like a dog.  While Jet was jumping, still being held by the harness on his back, Harry's arm was moving up and down like he was operating an old-fashioned water pump.  In retrospect, it was a funny sight, but, right then, we didn't have time to laugh.

Roger and I ran to assist.  I disconnected Jet from Harry, and, dropping to my knees, calmed him, while Roger took charge of Harry and pushed the tiddlywink back over the manhole.  After Harry and Jet were thoroughly calmed and reunited, Roger and I helped them into the back seat of the sedan, and drove them to Club Fifteen.

When I came back that evening, there wasn't a person there who hadn't heard the story, and I was greeted with a free draft beer and a round of applause.

Eventually, I was transferred to another division, became interested in other things, and lost track of Harry.  But, every once in a while I still wonder whatever happened to Jet and him.

AND . . . to this day . . . I have absolutely no idea what happened to my freshly starched shirts!

# What's Really Important?

**My work required me to ride a busy fire engine in a busy city with lots of traffic.** We tried to accommodate the traffic, as it wasn't kind to inconvenience folks when you could simply park closer to the curb, or move the hose a few feet and let folks drive by.

However, I lived in a not-so-busy city, on a road with single, one-way lanes separated by an island.

One Sunday morning, I went outside to start the car and run the A/C, so my wife wouldn't complain about the heat. There, in front of the house next door, was a fire engine, with hose running down the center of the road, in front of my house, then crossing the island to another engine, on the other side. The hose was flat, and, therefore dry, and the crew of that engine were simply sitting in the cab awaiting orders to "charge" the hose with water.

I walked up to the officer sitting in the right, front seat, and asked him if we could possibly move the hose to the side of the road, so I could back out and go to church. His immediate response was to threaten me with arrest.

Arrest? For asking him to accommodate a citizen, while the bum simply sat there with his thumb in his butt, and a dry hose running down the middle of the street? I never even started the car's engine; we simply stayed home, and I made breakfast.

It would have been easy for me to call the city mayor's office, the next day, or even my friend, the training officer for that guy's fire department—but I didn't. I simply wished that asshole a nice day, and went back inside my house.

If you think about it, that may have been that self-important asshole's one fire for the year. And, he was second in, sitting at a hydrant across the street, and down the block from the action. There he was, just waiting for orders and wishing he was over there at the fire.

Perhaps, if I had thought more deeply about it, I might have fired up my lawnmower and cut the neighbor's grass, throwing the clippings all over that lieutenant's brand new fire truck.

Oh, well, just one more missed opportunity!

Sam Stone

# Last Alarm

**For me, Charlie was the Fire Plug.  Round and hard, with calluses all the way to his elbows,** and seemingly put together with spring steel and barbed wire, he had the biggest, strongest hands I've ever seen.  He was afraid of nothing—definitely a blue collar, guts-up-front kinda guy.

Charlie hired on as a fireman (today, he'd be called a "Fire Fighter") during the final years of the old two-platoon, fire department.  Those guys stood roll call every morning, going on or off duty, and worked sixty-hour weeks.

Ten years later, the department had gone to three platoons and a minimum, five-man team on every truck.  I was the rookie, and the fourth guy on the tailboard of Engine Three.  In addition, there were Charlie, Dan, and Ronnie.  Our driver, Joe, and Lieutenant Eddie occupied the front seat.  My first three years, I was assigned to Engine Three, and learned a lot about fire fighting—and life—from those guys. Charlie once said, "Families may come and go, but the fire station is the one constant thing in your life."

Charlie grew up in Miami Beach, the lone Irish kid in a Jewish neighborhood. When the other boys went to Hebrew school, he tagged along. It took him very little time to master both Hebrew and Yiddish, much quicker than the others did—to the outspoken displeasure of the other kids' parents. By the time I came along, he also spoke fluent Spanish, and could get by in French, German, and Italian. He was a natural linguist, and his talents came in handy in the multicultural neighborhood surrounding old Station Three.

The term "fire plug" comes from the old days of wooden water mains. Arriving at a fire, a Fireman would dig down to the water main, and then drill a hole in it with an auger. The suction hose of the pumper had a tapered end that was driven into the hole, and through it the pumper drafted water from the water main to fight the fire. After the fire, a tapered hardwood dowel was hammered into the water main to "plug" the hole, and a mark was left on the curb identifying the location. The next time there was a fire on that street, they could dig down, pull the plug, and get right to work—thus the term "fire plug" was born.

Charlie was the guy who "squirted the clear stuff on the red stuff," and I backed him up. He would go all the way into a fire before opening the nozzle, and my ears would get so hot I could swear they were burning. I can't tell you how many times I swore if I lived through that fire I was never going to work with him again. BUT, charging into a fully involved building, with fire coming out of every window, is truly exciting, and when Charlie was on vacation, I got my share of time on the nozzle. I've said many times, "Dear God, please make Heaven a wood frame building, so hot you can see through it." (Once you've overcome the fear of fire, you can't get enough of it.)

Charlie developed cancer a few years ago, and it finally took its toll. Hospice was helping his wife, Joyce, care for him in their home, and the guys from Engine One came by almost daily to see if they could be of help. On his final Saturday, despite heavy drugs, he seemed to be having a particularly bad day, and was drifting in and out of consciousness, when Captain Jenkins and his crew swung by to say hello.

The sleeping giant opened his eyes, and, seeing the uniformed crew around his bed, he asked, "Am I late for roll call?"

Captain Jenkins laughed and said, "No, Charlie. You're right on time."

Charlie smiled and breathed his final breath.

Goodbye old friend, I thought. I've got your back. I'll see you at the next alarm.

# The River Rat

**The city of Miami is only twenty-three square miles,** but when folks talk about Miami, most often they're mistakenly including Coral Gables, Miami Beach, or one of the other outer areas as "The City." In the City itself, visitors are normally found in downtown, Coconut Grove, or perhaps driving Biscayne Boulevard. Otherwise, they stay on the Interstate and whiz right through.

My fire station was in the North End, a neighborhood now called "Little Haiti." In the late forties and early fifties, when I was a kid with dirt between my toes, the same neighborhood was known as "Little River." That's because the city ends at the Little River Canal, one of several waterways draining the Everglades that makes the land habitable. Little River was one of those communities that formed during the boom days. It was a busy "four-corners," with four banks, two bowling alleys, three movie theatres, lots of successful businesses—and a VFW post with WWI coastal artillery cannon out front (my brother and I spent hours operating the cranks that swung it around and elevated the barrel). One of the bowling alleys—and a movie theatre (both from the boom days)—had no roof. The bowling lanes were terrazzo.

We had our share of juvenile delinquents. One group was called the "Little River Rats." Its members were eight or nine years older than I was; they weren't really troublemakers, and mostly hung together and had fun. They were all truly tough enough that they didn't need to prove it.

Wally was a "Rat." Sixty-plus years later, he still had his "Rat" T-shirt. He was also a Fire Fighter, and was my lieutenant at Station Nine (and later, my captain at Station Five. I loved being the guy on the nozzle, and Wally knew it. He used to say, "You put the fire out, and I'll handle the paperwork." He was a wonderful leader.

There was another group of teenagers in Little River back then, about halfway between the ages of the Rats and me, a truly unpleasant group of lowlifes who called themselves "The Mice." Wally talked about how he and the Rats would catch a few Mice in an alley, now and again, and "beat 'em soft."

We had a place called The Youth Center. It was built by the local businessmen, who dedicated it to the city, to be used as a public parks building. It had a large assembly room; a game room with a half-dozen ping pong tables; rooms for ceramics and other activities; AND a full commercial kitchen with a huge, stainless steel refrigerator.

One day, Tony Luducio, a member of the Mice, decided he was going to shove me into the refrigerator. There I was, with my hands and feet planted on either side of the open door, and there was Tony, his shoulder pushed against the middle of my back, punching me in the kidneys. I was screaming bloody murder, and was certain of two things: one, Tony was eventually going to close me up in that refrigerator; and two, nobody was going to come to my aid.

Suddenly, an older teenager walked past the door to the kitchen and barked at Tony. In a flash, Tony dropped me on the floor and left me alone—for the rest of my life.

## Sam Stone

Some thirty-odd years later, I was sitting in the lobby of Station Five, with my feet on the watchman's desk, watching a Braves game, when Captain Wally joined me. For some reason, I thought about Tony Luducio and the refrigerator and told him the story. Without even looking my way, Wally said, "I told that bastid if he ever touched you again I was gonna break every bone in his body."

How do you thank someone who saved your life more than three quarters of a lifetime ago? I couldn't hold back. "Do you ever get tired of pulling my bacon out of the fire?"

Wally was silent for a moment, then finally looked up, smiled, and said (and I'll never forget it) "Ever day!"

# The Mercedes and
# the Fire Hydrant

**One of the first things I learned, early in my career as a firefighter,** is that it's kind of stupid to get into an argument with a fire hydrant—'cause you never win.

Jimmy Kay was driving Engine Four. Engine Three was first in at a warehouse fire, and needed a supply line. Arriving at the scene, we dropped off the lieutenant and two guys, who pulled the two-and-a-half-inch line, and I jumped on the sideboard, just as Jimmy dumped the clutch. We laid a line, nearly two blocks long, to the closest hydrant. Unfortunately, there was a brand new Mercedes right in front of it. Without hesitating, Jim came to a stop in the middle of the street, parallel to the Mercedes. "Get the axe and knock out the windows," he commanded. "I'll hook up the line." I just looked at him funny, and he pointed in the direction of the

Benz. "DO IT! We'll run the suction through the car."

So, I got the pike axe and shattered the windows on both sides. Now, this was in the good old days, long before large diameter, soft suction hoses, and, luckily, I had a lot more muscles than common sense, so I grabbed a ten-foot section of eight-inch, hard suction, manhandled it over to the car, and poked it through one window and out the other. I then removed the large cap from the hydrant and connected the huge brass adaptor.

Meanwhile, Jimmy, who was twice my size and strong as an ox, had the supply hose hooked up to Engine Four in no time, and grabbed the second suction off the truck like it was a toothpick. We rapidly connected it to the first section. Jimmy cautioned me not to tighten the coupling between the hoses, and, at the time, I didn't ask why. It took both of us to bend that big suction hose into a tight enough curve to enable it to be hooked up to the hydrant. The coupling between the two sections of hard suction was inside the car.

I opened the hydrant, and Jimmy began pumping water down the line to Engine Three. It felt like it took forever, but we eventually got water to Engine Three, before they emptied their tank— and that was important. That's when I noticed the coupling in the middle of the Mercedes was leaking water into the car. I grabbed the rubber mallet, climbed into the back seat, and began knocking the coupling tight. Jimmy yelled at me to make it even looser, because the guy needed to understand the penalty for parking in front of one of his hydrants— HIS hydrants—and maybe a car full of water would help him remember next time.

Typically, a police car is dispatched to a building fire, and one just happened to come around the corner, as the owner of the car came running out of the house, screaming and threatening to kill us for ruining his car. Well, that's all the encouragement the police officers needed, and, in a couple of heartbeats, the owner was locked in the back seat of the police car, with handcuffs on his ankles and wrists.

Later on, the paddy wagon came by, and the officers threw him into the back. I don't know what they're like now, but, back then, interiors of paddy wagons consisted simply of metal walls and a couple of metal benches, with nothing to hold onto. Before they threw the guy in, they connected the two sets of bracelets behind him, and he was now shaped like a big "O," with his ankles and wrists hooked together behind his back.

The paddy wagon took off with a lurch, went about a hundred yards, picking up speed, and suddenly the driver slammed on the brakes. Then, the process started all over again. I had the feeling that guy arrived at the city jail with lots of bruises.

All along, the coupling inside the car was leaking several gallons a minute. It's amazing how tight those cars are built, because it didn't take all that long before the whole thing was full of water, which finally began spilling out of the window openings. I'd be willing to bet the springs of that car were seriously damaged by all that weight. By the time it was all over, there had to have been somewhere near fifty cubic feet of water inside that car—and, at around sixty pounds per cubic foot, that's a lot of weight.

I never got to the fire that day, but I had a lot of fun at that hydrant. Lieutenant Cosgrove decided he didn't want anything to do with what happened at the hydrant, so he told Jimmy to make out the incident report as if he were the officer in charge. Jimmy wrote it out in longhand, and I typed it on the form.

When the District Chief came by to pick up the station's paper work that evening, he read the report aloud, looked at Jimmy and me for what felt like hours, then just turned around and left without saying another word, as Lieutenant Cosgrove stifled a laugh.

I sometimes wonder if the guy's insurance paid for the damage—or not!

Sam Stone

# The Three-Alarm Water Leak

**I was riding Ladder Nine, when we got dispatched to help Engine Nine with a water leak over by the bay.** The incident started with a small spring of water bubbling out of the alley, and, after taking a look, the supervisor from the water department decided that some installation across town was more important than a little leak. He told the owner of the apartment building they'd be back later to fix it.

It turned out what was leaking was a thirty-six inch, high pressure main, supplying the whole north end of Miami Beach. The inspector wasn't gone more than a couple of heartbeats, when the main blew a hole straight up off the top, and the alley erupted in a geyser four stories tall, throwing rocks the size of basketballs into the upper-story windows and onto the roof.

Engine Nine was dispatched first, and they eventually called for us. By the time we got there, the water was knee deep, and the electrical transformer on the pole near the leak was making all sorts of unfriendly noises. So, we immediately started evacuating everything on both sides of the alley—anything within a couple hundred feet of the geyser.

Captain Jenkins keeps a metal box full of notes in the dash of the ladder truck. He opened it, removed a small notebook, turned a few pages, and told George and me to follow him to the intersection with a water key and a pry bar. For those of you who don't know, a water key is a steel rod about five feet long, with a two-foot, tee handle welded to one end and a two-inch square welded to the other. It works better with two men than one.

The captain looked around, got his bearings, and took the key, knocking it into the street under all that water, going *glub, glub, glub,* when suddenly there was a metal clang. He told us to pop the "tiddlywink" (some folks call it a manhole cover) and shut off the valve beneath it. While we were doing that, he took two guys from Engine Nine to the other end of the block, and did the same thing. We had the leak stopped in less than ten minutes—while those guys from the engine had been standing around with their thumbs up their asses for nearly an hour before we were even dispatched!

So there we were, standing around congratulating ourselves, when the transformer on the power pole next to the hole in the ground started making some really nasty noises. Next thing we knew, it blew up and blinded most of us because we were looking straight at it. (Electrical transformers are full of oil, and when they blow, it's like a small bomb exploding.)

When my vision returned, there was fire in one apartment on the second floor, and two on the third floor. That's when the captain called for a building fire assignment, and they sent us another engine, a rescue, and a district chief.

The apartment building closest to the transformer had open walkways facing the alley. We thought we had evacuated all the apartments, but suddenly a young couple came running out of one next to the second-floor fire. The girl was wrapped in a blanket that covered . . . well . . . almost everything, and the guy was pulling his pants up as they ran.

Eventually, one of the weasels from the city attorney's office showed up. He was talking to the owner (trying to deny responsibility) and he asked him to sign some sort of paper releasing the city from any financial obligation.

George interrupted them to ask the owner to unlock a door on the other side of the building. While they were out of sight of the attorney, he told the owner not to make any kind of a deal until after he'd seen his own attorney. So, when the owner got back to the city attorney, he refused to sign anything and the attorney went berserk. That's when Captain Jenkins hauled the attorney down the stairs and stuffed him into his car.

About that same time, the water department inspector returned, and the captain had fun screaming at him.

In all, it was one hell of an afternoon—with all the fire and flood we could ask for. The only thing missing was a hurricane!

Made in the USA
Coppell, TX
10 February 2022

73371498R00075